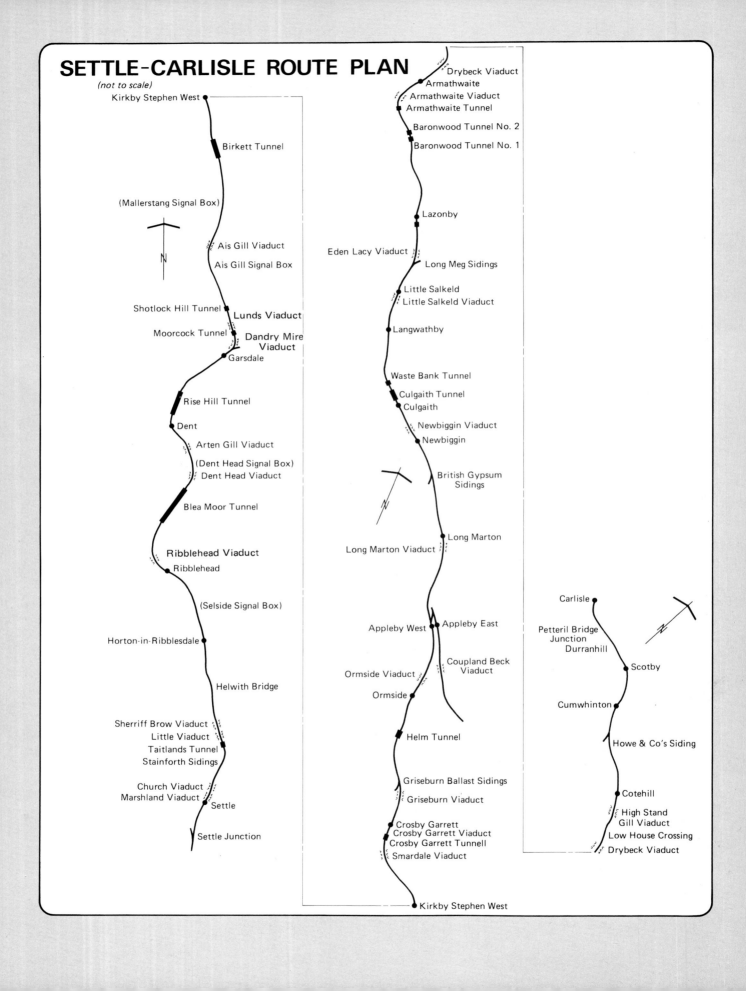

SETTLE-CARLISLE ROUTE PLAN

(not to scale)

Kirkby Stephen West

Birkett Tunnel

(Mallerstang Signal Box)

Ais Gill Viaduct
Ais Gill Signal Box

Shotlock Hill Tunnel
Lunds Viaduct
Moorcock Tunnel
Dandry Mire Viaduct
Garsdale

Rise Hill Tunnel
Dent
Arten Gill Viaduct
(Dent Head Signal Box)
Dent Head Viaduct

Blea Moor Tunnel

Ribblehead Viaduct
Ribblehead

(Selside Signal Box)

Horton-in-Ribblesdale

Helwith Bridge

Sherriff Brow Viaduct
Little Viaduct
Taitlands Tunnel
Stainforth Sidings

Church Viaduct
Marshland Viaduct
Settle

Settle Junction

Drybeck Viaduct
Armathwaite
Armathwaite Viaduct
Armathwaite Tunnel
Baronwood Tunnel No. 2
Baronwood Tunnel No. 1

Lazonby

Eden Lacy Viaduct
Long Meg Sidings

Little Salkeld
Little Salkeld Viaduct

Langwathby

Waste Bank Tunnel
Culgaith Tunnel
Culgaith
Newbiggin Viaduct
Newbiggin

British Gypsum Sidings

Long Marton
Long Marton Viaduct

Appleby West   Appleby East

Coupland Beck Viaduct

Ormside Viaduct
Ormside

Helm Tunnel

Griseburn Ballast Sidings

Griseburn Viaduct

Crosby Garrett
Crosby Garrett Viaduct
Crosby Garrett Tunnell
Smardale Viaduct

Kirkby Stephen West

Carlisle

Petteril Bridge
Junction
Durranhill

Scotby

Cumwhinton

Howe & Co's Siding

Cotehill
High Stand
Gill Viaduct
Low House Crossing
Drybeck Viaduct

DIESELS OVER THE SETTLE TO CARLISLE ROUTE

Peter Walton

Printed and bound in the City of Oxford

ACKNOWLEDGEMENTS

My thanks go to all those people who have assisted in the preparation of this book, with especial thanks going to Mr. M. Karrier, the management and staff of British Rail, Liz, parents and friends, and a very patient Sylvia for the typing.

Published by:
Oxford Publishing Co.,
8 The Roundway,
Headington, Oxford.

DEDICATION

To the memory of my dog, Magic, whose company I shall remember forever.

Photographic note:
All photographs in this book have been taken using the following equipment:

Ross Ensign
Rolleicord

and latterly, two excellent Canons, an FX and F1 complete with supplementary Soligor preset lenses.

Introduction

The Settle to Carlisle Railway, via which the Midland Railway Company eventually forged its way to Scotland during the 1870s, has always held a unique attraction for railway enthusiasts. This route should never have been chosen. Of all the logical ways to the North, the bleak fells of Westmorland and North Yorkshire should have been a late choice but the Midland had little option. The resultant route, therefore, possessed more than its fair share of natural obstacles, which were to be overcome, and gave rise to the marvellous and ambitious engineering works still evident today.

For 90 years, steam locomotives toiled over 'The Long Drag' providing a third route to Scotland. But during the 50s and 60s, the character of the line changed with the emergence of the diesel engine. Ironically, this period produced a galaxy of glorious motive power over the Settle to Carlisle route to serve the final rites of steam; 'A3s', 'A1s', 'Scots', 'Jubilees', 'Patriots', 'Britannias' and 'Clans'; 'Black 5s, 'Fowler 4s', 'Ivatt 3s', '8Fs', '9Fs' and many more were commonplace during the early 1960s. After 11th August 1968, steam was no more, the transition was complete and the Settle to Carlisle line moved into the diesel age.

From the early 1960s, diesel haulage on regular expresses had become the 'norm'. Class 45s, then called 'Peaks', invariably D14—D32 from Leeds Holbeck depot, handled the 'Thames—Clyde' and 'Waverley' expresses, plus the morning 'down' Leeds to Glasgow and the afternoon 'up' return. The Leeds to Glasgow working, now altered to start from Nottingham Midland, still operates basically unchanged. The through workings from London however, have, regrettably, been withdrawn, the 'Waverley' being a significant casualty, taking with it the splendid North British route from Carlisle to Edinburgh. The withdrawal of the 'Thames—Clyde' signalled the end for the last through working from London St. Pancras to Glasgow.

A new timetable and working pattern evolved during the early 1970s, in essence, a reasonable alternative to the previous workings; namely, three 'down' and three 'up' expresses per day. This timetable is reproduced as Appendix 1.

The existing Nottingham—Carlisle expresses will begin to run through to Glasgow Central from the start of the new 1980 timetable. Generally encouraging 'passengers carried' figures during the late 1970s could perhaps tempt speculation that a direct London connection may, one day, be reinstated.

The exclusive preserve of the Class 45s has been progressively challenged by the infiltration of Class 40s and 47s, to such an extent that during period of 1979, in particular, there was a healthy mixture of the three basic types to be seen on the Settle—Carlisle expresses.

The pattern of freight working has changed little since steam days, with the exception of gradual withdrawal of pick up/local services, and the total loss of such as the 'Long Meg' anhydrite trains. Former crew change/watering points have disappeared. Present day freights arrive via Blackburn or via Leeds, from places as far away as Cornwall, Severn Tunnel Junction and Parkeston Quay, and Class 25s, 40s, 45s and 47s are common sights on the freights of today.

The detailed history of the Settle—Carlisle Railway is well documented in many previous publications, opening and closing dates, building details, locomotive performances etc. It is not the aim of this book to duplicate this information, but in association with the route map at the start of the book, the text and accompanying photographs describe more recent activities and occurrences, creating a picture of life on the Settle—Carlisle route in the diesel age, right up to the present day.

Although so much has been written about the Settle—Carlisle line, certain areas of operation have been neglected. Of these, the vital role of the ubiquitous Midland style signal box is noticeable. Accordingly, photographs of many of these and a résumé of the existing signalling (Appendix 5) are included. From a photographic point of view, I have tried to concentrate, geographically, upon areas which have, hitherto, often received scant coverage; namely the excellent stretches of line between Ais Gill and Armathwaite.

A stranger to the Midland, Class 47, No. 47 077 *North Star* eases round the curve over Armathwaite Viaduct with the afternoon 'down' express, on 10th November 1979.

Brief Topography of the Present Day Settle Junction to Carlisle; Line and Installations

Settle Junction once boasted a station and two signal boxes. Now the station has disappeared and only one box controls the junction. The siting of the junction and the track layout has changed considerably over the years, the last notable alteration being made during 1979, following the serious derailment which occurred in the spring of that year, when approximately 40 wagons were involved. The line to Giggleswick and the West falls away from the Settle line, which continues northwards into Settle station. A hand painted and decorated board, extolling the virtues of the Yorkshire Dales and indicating distances to North and South, is displayed on the 'up' platform; a legacy from the days of Stationmaster Taylor.

Ascending from Settle over viaducts and rivers towards Horton, the railway passes the site of Stainforth signal box and sidings on the East side of the line. It continues to climb steadily northwards through Taitlands Tunnel and then traverses the short level stretch at Helwith Bridge, (the box for the quarry is now demolished), before gaining height, almost continuously, to Blea Moor Tunnel.

Horton-in-Ribblesdale signal box still serves the quarry at Horton. The station here, again once worked by Stationmaster Taylor, also had an attractive name board prior to closure, but alas, it has disappeared.

Today, Horton station is used only by 'Dalesrail' passengers. The 'Dalesrail' system seems to have set a healthy precedent throughout the Settle—Carlisle system and some details of its operation can be found in Appendix 2.

The isolated cabin at Selside was closed relatively recently and removed to Carnforth. The original sign from Selside signal box was fixed to the East facing front; when removed and replaced by North and South facing signs, the original sign was fixed to a building in the village of Selside.

Ribblehead station, and the reconnected quarry siding, is reached at a little over 1,000 ft above sea level, the quarry siding generating traffic for the South and being controlled by Blea Moor signal box. Unfortunately, in order to achieve the re-connection of the quarry, the Ribblehead 'down' platform was demolished. 'Dalesrail' operation tends to suffer from the absence of this platform.

Battymoss viaduct spans the famous 'dry valley'. Much has already been written of this terrific structure, as impressive today as ever. Its structural maintenance continues to cause concern, and it is almost constantly under repair.

Blea Moor signal box, recently deprived of two of its accompanying cottages and watering facilities, still remains as one of the most important points on the line. Now one of the loneliest boxes in the land, it remains open, under normal circumstances, 24 hours a day.

The line plunges through a short tunnel prior to being committed to the depths of Blea Moor Tunnel itself; host to so many tragedies whilst under construction, it still succeeds in exuding a thoroughly forbidding atmosphere. Who knows what ghosts still lurk in and around this grim hole?

From the gloom the track bursts out into slightly less barren countryside and crosses Dent Head Viaduct. The box, now demolished, stood on the West side of the line,

North of the viaduct. The lovely viaduct at Arten Gill is crossed and the railway skirts the underside of the semi-derelict snow fencing, high above Dentdale.

Dent signal box, still in nice condition, set against a cluster of buildings, is sited immediately to the South of the station and lonely Stationmaster's house. The station is now a weekend retreat for a school in Lancashire, a far cry from the neatness and tidiness evident here when it was proudly claimed to be the highest mainline station in England, following the demise of its not too distant neighbour at Barras on the dramatic Stainmore route.

The exit from Dent, beneath an unusual overbridge carrying a stream, is followed by two semaphore distant signals on the 'up' and the Rise Hill Tunnel. Emergence from Rise Hill reveals the beautiful valley of Grisedale to the West as the line clings to the fellside, swinging round to Garsdale over the site of the highest water troughs in England. Garsdale station was formerly the junction for Hawes and thence the North East via Northallerton.

The station buildings and platform signal box remain, as does the pit, and part of the famous turntable. The water tower and cranes have been demolished. Typical Midland Railway cottages exist on the West side of the station, and about half a mile again on the East, immediately after crossing Dandry Mire viaduct, from which the track bed of the Hawes branch can easily be seen diverging to the East.

The track next negotiates Moorcock Tunnel through to Lunds, over the viaduct and under the footbridge, near the site of the tragic crash of 1910. Shotlock Hill Tunnel follows, the highest tunnel in England, and then Ais Gill 'down' distant signal, framed by the famous and impressive bulk of Wild Boar Fell. Ais Gill signal box is now normally closed, and the summit is indicated by the one remaining summit board as being 1,169 ft above sea level. The line immediately descends past angry waterfalls to East and West, under the road bridge and over the much photographed Ais Gill Viaduct. A number of well preserved timber farm overbridges exist on the sweep through Mallerstang, the box there having long ago been destroyed by fire.

Preceded by a graceful overbridge, Birkett Tunnel allows the line to pass through Wharton Fell and introduces it to progressively friendly terrain high above Kirkby Stephen. Kirkby Stephen West station, recently shorn of its 'down' waiting room, still possesses a Goods Shed, which is still in use by a local haulage contractor, and a signal box which replaced an earlier structure. Midland Railway property surrounds the road overbridge as the line descends towards the rock cutting at Waitby and then the lovely viaduct at Smardale.

A glimpse of the superb North Eastern Viaduct, straddling Scandal Beck further to the West, can be stolen at the northern end of the Midland Smardale Viaduct, as in fact, can one of the much overgrown track bed of the North Eastern Railway from Smardale station to the East, as it passes underneath the Midland Viaduct. It was here that a link was once proposed, from Midland to North Eastern, which would have joined Kirkby Stephen West to Kirkby Stephen East stations.

Plate 1 Class 40, No. 40 003 accelerates away from Leeds City's platform 8, on 28th August 1979, with the 10.25 Nottingham—Glasgow express. A foretaste of things to come.

Plate 2 Class 45, No. 12, now renumbered 45 011, awaits departure from Leeds City. The reporting code for the 07.15 Nottingham—Glasgow express, 1S49, is now no longer displayed on the front of locomotives.

Crosby Garrett Tunnel accepts the line once the crossing of Smardale has been completed. Crosby Garrett Viaduct carries it safely over the village bearing the same name, and through the site of the unique station which closed in the 1950s. The signal box here lasted well into the 60s but has now succumbed, as have almost all readily identifiable signs of the activity that was Crosby Garrett.

Griseburn Ballast Siding signal box is in excellent condition. There are also two semi-detached bungalows which once provided accommodation for the Griseburn signalmen. Further descent over the massive embankment, near Breaks Hall, prepares the way for Helm Tunnel, named after the famous wind which sweeps over the Pennines and which creates the 'Helm Bar' cloud formation.

At Ormside, the line passes through the station, long since closed and now suffering a similar fate to that of Dent. The 'up' side waiting room and platform have been demolished, and the signal box and siding removed, although the track bed is remarkably well preserved. Ormside Viaduct follows and the A66 is crossed. At this stage, the former N E R Eden Valley branch can be seen, to the East, entering Appleby parallel with the Midland line.

Express Dairy once despatched its 'Milk for London' from private sidings, South of Appleby, the sidings being controlled by a ground frame box operated from Appleby West box. Siding and ground frame are now gone, but the site of both can be seen to the East of the line as Appleby is approached. The goods yard here is lifted and the most important intermediate box on the line, Appleby West, has been removed almost without trace. The goods shed, presently the home of a small engineering concern, is well preserved. The shunter's cabin, once the haunt of Shunter Tommy Blaylock, was demolished during the 'clear up' for Bishop Eric Treacy's Memorial Service in 1978. This 'shunters' cabin was known to older railwaymen by the name 'Butching Shed'. Apparently, cattle for London's Bishopsgate Market were slaughtered and despatched from here long ago. Photographs of some other 'cabin casualties' are included. The water tower and cranes have gone, but the station itself remains in good repair, unfortunately marred by unsympathetic and expensive platform lighting of the same style which spoils Settle station. The name 'Appleby' appears on the embankment behind the 'up' platform in large letters made of stones. The name was formerly displayed using daffodils. The North signal box remains, and controls entrance/exit to the Engineers' sidings, the truncated section of the Eden Valley branch to Warcop, and, of course, main line activities. The area behind the North box, occupied by engineers establishments, boasts some attractive cabins and sheds in timber, brick and stone. Regrettably the turntable disappeared during the 1960s.

The North Eastern Railways Eden Valley branch, once part of a splendid system centring on Kirkby Stephen East, deserves a book on its own. The only remaining part, however, is generally grouped as an integral section of the Settle—Carlisle route. The access to the branch is via the link behind Appleby North box. Appleby West Junction box, not to be confused with Appleby West (Midland), controlled the Midland to North Eastern Junction at the East end of this link. The signalling and box have since gone. Double track, now singled, took the line to the decorative station at Appleby East where the main buildings remain in a semi-derelict state. A North Eastern Railway lattice post signal, minus arms, still survives, as does the Goods Shed which has become the local bus garage. The line proceeds through five miles of the Eden Valley, over Coupland Beck Viaduct, to Warcop, where remains of the beautiful station and platform signal box can still be appreciated and runround facilities still exist. The line is severed between Warcop and Flitholme Cabin (signal post Warcop No. 13). The section between Warcop and Merrygill Quarry survived until 1974, when, despite protests about the ruination of village life in Hartley and Winton by heavy lorries, the traffic was stripped from the railway.

Back to the main line, which now passes the Engineers' sidings and crosses over the new concrete bridge which integrates with the construction of Appleby by-pass. This by-pass regrettably obliterates some signs of the NER branch to Penrith which once crossed under the Midland at this point. Beneath the Roman Road bridge, past Croft Ends, the line swings North over Longmarton Viaduct and through Longmarton.

The station here is semi-derelict, the signal box has gone but the sandstone Goods Shed remains. Longmarton was once the collection point for Byrites delivered via overhead ropeway and loaded into wagons near the Goods Shed. British Gypsum, Kirkby Thore, despatches goods, via rail, from private sidings controlled by a ground frame between Long Marton and Newbiggin. The daily 'pick-up', 9T35 from Carlisle, serves British Gypsum and Warcop as required, its eventual destination being Oxwell Mains near Dunbar. The 'pick-up' is also responsible for a series of tasks, legacies from the history of the Settle—Carlisle, conveying paraffin to Long Meg, coal to the boxes, etc. In similar fashion, 7E84, the 07.30 Carlisle—Tinsley, picks up water-cans at Appleby for Blea Moor, and empties to take to Skipton from whence they are returned to Appleby for refilling.

Newbiggin station retains a semi-derelict timber waiting room on the 'down' platform. The main station building is more or less intact, but the box and goods yards are no more. Facilities for the limited movement of wagons by rope and pulley once existed at Newbiggin as despatch points for trains from British Gypsum. Newbiggin Viaduct comes next and then the highest three arch bridge on the line, before the curve into Culgaith. There is a fine signal box here in lovely condition, but unfortunately it is now equipped with modern crossing barriers. The unique 'up' side station building has been converted into a private dwelling, and the 'down' side timber platform and waiting room have been removed completely. Two short tunnels follow, and then the line emerges into the open above the impressive confluence of the Rivers Eamont and Eden.

The railway passes beneath, in quick succession, three Midland overbridges, and eventually reaches Langwathby. The station buildings and Goods Shed remain, but the signal box and goods yard are demolished. The signal box, large and impressive, was once presided over by Signalman Strong who kept the interior spotless. Geraniums, in two rows, graced the glass frontage and everything was polished to perfection. The stone slab under the coal stove was painted white, and any ash which marked the stone was immediately removed, and the affected area 'touched up' with a white concoction from a jam jar. All, alas, is now just a memory.

Little Salkeld Viaduct signals the approach to Little Salkeld station. The 'up' side main building survives complete with 'up' and 'down' side platforms, but again the signal box and yards, etc. have vanished.

Long Meg signal box, of the modern type, controls the siding and loop facilities, but the despatch area for the famous Long Meg—Widnes anhydrite trains has been lifted.

Plate 3 The original 'Peaks' were involved in a number of test trains over parts of the Settle—Carlisle route shortly after their introduction. Unfortunately, few photographs of any of the original batch of locomotives at work in this way survive. Here No. D10 *Tryfan* speeds through Tring Cutting.

B. Cooper

Eden Lacy Viaduct, overlooked by interesting caves, takes the Midland over the Eden and towards Lazonby, past disused quarries to the East, followed immediately by the short Lazonby Tunnel and Lazonby station, one of the best preserved on the line, and formerly one of the most important, as a result of Lazonby's livestock auctions and the close proximity of the village to the station.

As an example of its importance, the staff employed at Lazonby during the Second World War were as follows:

Stationmaster	:	Joe Brunskill
Clerk	:	Dick Harper
2 Goods Shed/	:	Jimmy Bell &
Station Porters	:	Teddy Glendinning
Cattle Dock Man	:	Johnny Graham
Junior Porter	:	Alan Dugdale

Main buildings survive as do lamp standards, water tower and 'down' side water-crane, goods shed and 'up' side waiting room. The signal box and goods yard have been removed. Leaving Lazonby the pump house for watering facilities may be seen to the East by the stream side.

The run towards Armathwaite through wooded gorges and tunnels is most attractive. The tunnels in Baronwood bracket the little ground frame box and siding which once enabled the despatch of Christmas trees from the surrounding woodland, and also the receipt of coals, etc. for the local estate.

The viaduct at Coomb Eden is crossed before passing Armathwaite, and here the station has been extensively modernised to form a community centre. Signal box, 'up' side waiting room, platforms and goods shed still stand. The exit from Armathwaite over Drybeck Viaduct sweeps past the little box at Low House Crossing. Cotehill station has disappeared, almost without trace, and the site is marked by the presence of some railway dwellings immediately to the North of High Stand Gill Viaduct.

Howe and Company signal box is the fringe box for Carlisle, and this box controls the access to a private siding. Cumwhinton station is remarkably well preserved, despite its closure in 1952, with the 'up' and 'down' side station buildings remaining complete with their platforms.

Scotby station is slightly less fortunate, although the 'down' side main building survives as a private dwelling.

The eventual merge with the NER Newcastle—Carlisle line at Petteril Bridge Junction, occurs shortly beyond the site of Durranhill signal box and the former Midland shed at Durranhill.

Finally, two lines run under London Road and join with the West Coast Main Line for the last few yards into Carlisle Citadel station.

Plate 4   Settle Junction signal box.

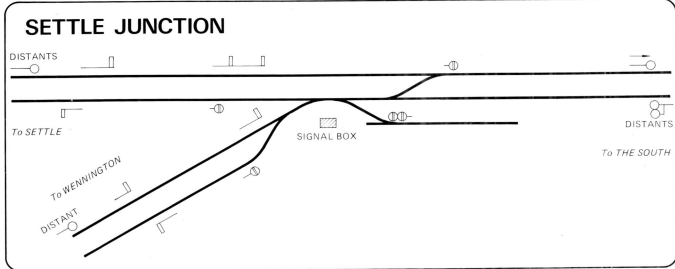

SETTLE JUNCTION

DISTANTS

To SETTLE

To WENNINGTON

DISTANT

SIGNAL BOX

DISTANTS

To THE SOUTH

Plate 5 *(above)* No. 40 131 coasts through Settle with an 'up' ballast train on 21st March 1980.

Plate 6 *(below)* Class 46, No. 46 035, waits for time at Settle station, after a superb run from Appleby in 34 minutes and 40 seconds (start to stop) with the lightweight 09.35 Carlisle–Nottingham express service.

Plate 9 The permanent way gangers post box at Settle station.

Plate 7 Monica Potter, of Settle fame, converses with the guard of the morning Carlisle—Nottingham express.

SETTLE   CARLISLE

MIDLAND RAILWAY EXTENSION

OPENED TO PASSENGERS - 1 MAY 1876

Plate 8 The decorative nameboard on Settle station 'up' platform still in existence in March 1980.

Plate 10 *(above)* The fine style of building, as seen on the line, is typified in this photograph of Settle station Main building, from the road access.

Plate 11 *(below)* The same buildings, but this time photographed from the platform side.

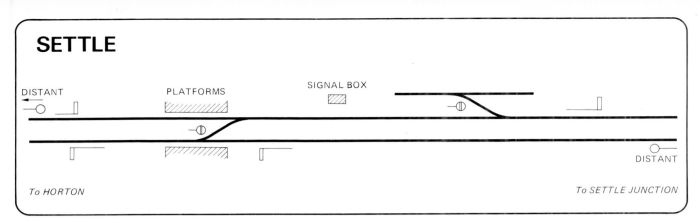

SETTLE

DISTANT   PLATFORMS   SIGNAL BOX

To HORTON   To SETTLE JUNCTION

DISTANT

Plate 12 *(above)* The mammoth structure of the goods shed and office is well portrayed in this photograph, and, again, is typical of the type of stone and architecture of the line. Notice the brackets for the, now missing, fire buckets on the small office wall.

Plate 13 *(right)* The massive beams and iron work of the goods shed roof are shown in this photograph. Note the platform edge supporting stones.

Plate 14 Horton signal box showing well the style of construction typical of all the boxes on the line.

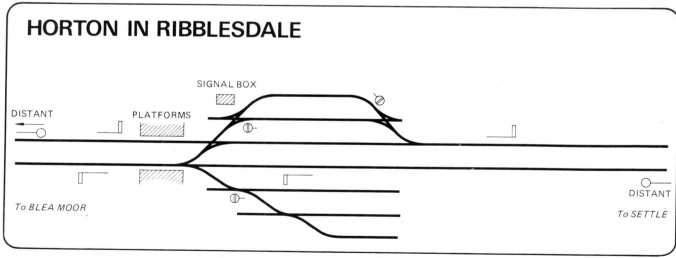

HORTON IN RIBBLESDALE

DISTANT

PLATFORMS

SIGNAL BOX

To BLEA MOOR

DISTANT

To SETTLE

Plate 15 *(left, above)* Activity at Horton as an unidentified ▶
Class 31 shunts with an engineers' train in March 1980.

Plate 16 *(left, below)* Ribblehead ballast empties on their ▶
way through Horton on 25th March 1980, with Class 25,
No. 25 276, in charge.

Plate 17 *(above)* A Class 40, No. 40 109, drifts southwards, overlooked by the snowy bulk of Penyghent, on 31st December 1979.

Plate 18 *(below)* A Class 31, No. 31 272, arrives at the ground frame at Ribblehead, with an assortment of hopper wagons.

Plate 19 *(right)* The same train as in the previous plate, but this time backing cautiously up into the relief line.

Plate 20 Amid complete stillness, after the snow storm, we see an unidentified Class 45 proceeding quietly through the station at Ribblehead, with a mixed goods train on 31st December 1979.

Plate 21   A lengthy freight descends, amid complete snow desolation, from Blea Moor over Batty Moss Viaduct on 31st December 1979. Note the scaffolding around the viaduct, confirming the problems the line is facing with ever increasing masonry repairs.

Plate 22   The same train approaches Ribblehead station, which is overshadowed by Whernside. It is of interest that there are three tents in the field, presumably occupied by 'late' campers or walkers.

Plate 23 *(above)* With a flash, the sunlight catches the screen of Class 45, No. 45 005, as it slows on approaching the slack over Batty Moss Viaduct on 12th April 1980.

Plate 24 *(right)* The Blea Moor 'up' water crane, having been much in demand in its time, now rusts away, minus its canvas pipe. Note the 'fire devil' and simple water tap.

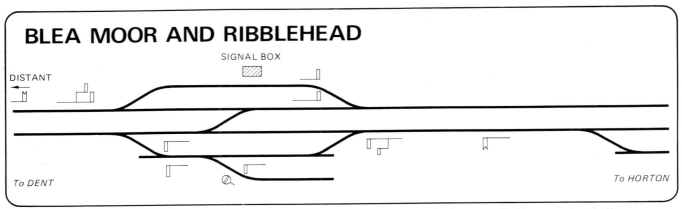

BLEA MOOR AND RIBBLEHEAD

SIGNAL BOX

DISTANT

To DENT

To HORTON

Plate 25 The loneliest box on the line is Blea Moor. This box controls the two relief loops and main line cross-over. It is different in construction to the others on the line and certainly looks more robust, enabling it to withstand the snow, winds and rain.

BLEA MOOR

Plate 26 With a gas lamp still hanging from the ceiling, this photograph, taken in 1979, shows the compact interior of Blea Moor signal box.

Plate 29 Dent Head signal box (with windows smashed), awaits its final fate, after many years of service.

Plate 27 *(left, upper)* The track layout at Blea Moor is well shown in this picture. The two loops, protected by catch points, and the main line cross-over are visible. Two cottages and a water tower, which once stood here, have now been demolished.

Plate 28 *(left, lower)* Dent Head Viaduct as seen from the slopes above the northern portal of Blea Moor Tunnel. In an attempt to break up the vast wilderness, note the hundreds of young trees which have been planted during recent years.

Plate 30 *(below)* Class 40, No. 40 098, wends its way through the snowbound cuttings south of Arten Gill with a down freight on 17th March 1980.

Plate 31 *(right, above)* Crossing Arten Gill Viaduct on 17th March 1980 with a down mixed freight is ▶ Class 40, No. 40 109. The mixture of wagons can be well seen, with seven new ambulances en route to the south.

Plate 32 *(right, below)* A welcome period of hazy sunshine greets Class 40, No. 40 196, in charge of an 'up' ▶ freight, as it leaves Arten Gill Viaduct on 17th March 1980.

Plate 33 *(below)* On 22nd April 1976, we find Class 47, No. 47 444, with full power being applied, between Arten Gill Viaduct and Dent. The fine construction of the viaduct can be clearly seen on the right.

Plate 34 *(right, upper)* Class 45, No. 45 038, speeds through Dentdale with the 11.50 Glasgow Central— ▶
Nottingham express on 15th September 1979.

Plate 35 *(right, lower)* Class 40, No. 40 025 *Lusitania* cants over as it rounds the curve through Dent, ▶
with an up mixed freight on 17th March 1980. Note the bands on the signal post to help identify against the snowy background.

Plate 36 Here we see Dent Station signal box with its lower windows 'grilled' to stop ballast breaking them.

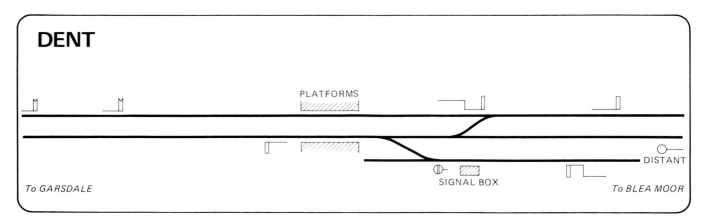

Plate 37 *(right, upper)* A Class 25, No. 25 201, works 'wrong line' with an engineers' train near the site of ▶ Garsdale troughs on 18th February 1978.

Plate 38 *(right, lower)* A Class 45 eases gently through Garsdale on the 07.15 Nottingham—Glasgow ▶ express.

Plate 39 *(above)* This photograph shows the all-wooden construction of Garsdale signal box, which is situated on the station platform. Note the crow perched on the signal arm.

Plate 41 *(right)* A further look at the track and block instruments in the box at Garsdale.

Plate 40 *(below)* The block shelf of Garsdale signal box.

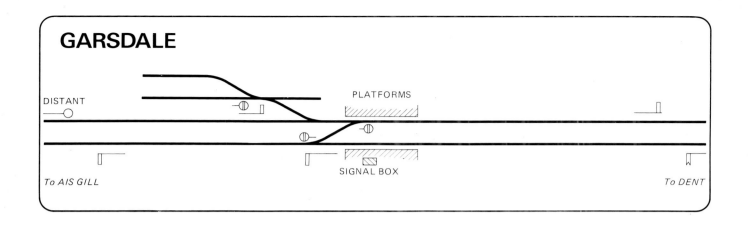

GARSDALE

DISTANT

PLATFORMS

SIGNAL BOX

To AIS GILL

To DENT

Plate 42 Class 47, No. 47 469, sweeps over Dandry Mire Viaduct towards Garsdale with 1M70, the 09.35 Carlisle–Nottingham express, whilst a Class 40 approaches with 1S49, the 07.15 Nottingham-Glasgow express.

Ivan Welsh

Plate 43 *(left)* Running off the Dandry Mire Viaduct, is Class 45, No. 45 134, with the 11.50 Glasgow—Nottingham express on 6th October 1979.

Plate 44 *(below)* Class 25, No. 25 075, unofficially named *Ballachulish*, is running late and in trouble on Dandry Mire Viaduct, with an excursion composed of special stock, on 6th October 1979. The desolation of the area is well portrayed in this photograph.

Plate 45 *(right)* A Class 45, on a down mixed freight, traverses Dandry Mire Viaduct during 1975.

Plate 46 *(below)* Garsdale sunset, in March 1980.

Plate 47 *(left)* With a diverted 'up' express, a Class 47 sweeps over Lunds Viaduct towards Moorcock Tunnel. Note the footbridge in the distance.

Plate 48 *(below)* The engine is kicking up snow and icicles hang in the damp tunnel, as a Class 45 plunges into the short tunnel at Shotlock Hill with the 07.15 Nottingham to Glasgow express on 31st December 1979.

Plate 49 *(right)* In charge of the 07.15 Nottingham—Glasgow express is No. 45 019, pictured between Lunds and Shotlock Hill Tunnel. The footbridge, shown in *Plate 47*, can be seen in the background.

Plate 50 *(below)* Class 47, No. 47 050, on time, with the 09.35 Carlisle—Nottingham express between Ais Gill and Shotlock Hill Tunnel on 31st December 1979.

I. Welsh

Plate 51 *(left, upper)* Class 40, No. 40 120, with front number, precedes the morning 'up' express with an 'up' freight, between Ais Gill and Shotlock Hill Tunnel, on 31st December 1979.

Plate 52 *(left, lower)* The summit is almost in sight for the 09.15 Euston—Glasgow express, passing Ais Gill Down Distant signal, headed by a Class 47. Ais Gill, and some of the other boxes to the south, still possessed semaphore Distant signalling at this time.

Plate 53 *(above)* A Class 50 wanders through Ais Gill on its way to Blea Moor. It will remain there for most of the day, acting as standby relief engine for the batch of re-routed West Coast Main Line expresses which will be diverted over the Settle—Carlisle route during winter Sundays.

Plate 56 *(above)* Another view of Class 40, No. 40 132, stranded at Ais Gill.

P. Holden

Plate 57 *(right)* Ais Gill signal box, devoid of signboards and 'up' refuge sidings, shields the quiet approach of a Class 47 on the 09.15 Euston—Glasgow Central express.

◄ **Plate 54** *(left, upper)* Class 50, No. 50 040 runs through bleak Ais Gill on 19th January 1975 with 1S61, the Birmingham—Glasgow express.

◄ **Plate 55** *(left, lower)* Winters are wild on the Settle and Carlisle, and here is a typical scene during winter months. Being released at Ais Gill, probably only to proceed to the next depot, is Class 40, No. 40 132.

P. Holden

Plate 58   Ais Gill signal box, in blizzard conditions, on 19th January 1975.

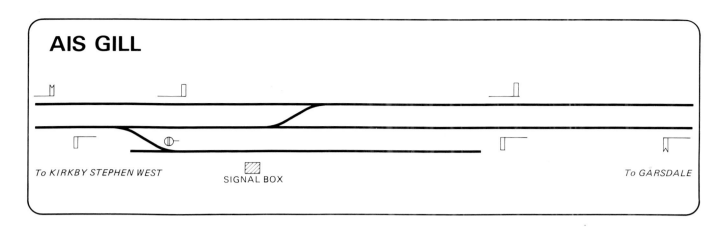

AIS GILL

To KIRKBY STEPHEN WEST

SIGNAL BOX

To GARSDALE

Plate 59 Class 40, No. 40 192, climbs the last few yards to Ais Gill summit, past the 260 milepost, with a mixed freight, on 22nd April 1976.

Plate 60 *(above)* A lone enthusiast photographs a Class 47 on the 09.40 Liverpool Lime Street—Glasgow Central express, as it rushes past Ais Gill 'up' Distant signal and begins the descent through Mallerstang.

Plate 61 *(left)* Trains meet north of Ais Gill. A Class 40 slips down the gradient whilst a Class 47 powers up the approach to the summit.

Plate 62 *(right, upper)* A Class 50 toils up the last stretch of the 1 in 100 gradient, near Ais Gill Viaduct, on 19th January 1975, with the 09.25 Glasgow—Birmingham New Street express.

Plate 63 *(right, lower)* Class 37, No. 37 081, with an engineers' train, clatters through Mallerstang on a glorious Saturday morning, 15th September 1979, bound for Garsdale.

Plate 64 Mallerstang signal box, now demolished, sitting high above Outhgill in the early 1960s.

S. Steadman

Plate 65 *(above)* Bidding farewell to Mallerstang, and preparing to enter Birkett Tunnel, is Class 40, No. 40 162, on 20th May 1978, with the 07.15 Nottingham—Glasgow express.

Plate 66 *(right)* Class 45, No. 45 040 *King's Shropshire Light Infantry* exits from Birkett Tunnel with a 'down' express.

Plate 69 *(right, upper)* Attacking ▶
the climb to Ais Gill in fine style
after a signal check at Kirkby
Stephen West, is Class 40, No.
40 010 *Empress of Britain.* The
train is 1Z76, an Edinburgh—
Swansea, returning Rugby match
excursion, nearing Birkett Tunnel
on 21st January 1979.

Plate 70 *(right, lower)* Snarling at ▶
the bank, No. 40 008 shatters the
peace of Wharton Hall on 27th
July 1979 whilst heading the 16.10
Glasgow Central to Nottingham
express.

Plate 67 *(left)* The 08.20 e.c.s.
Glasgow to Red Bank hurries
towards Birkett Tunnel and the
south. This train, 5M20, unless
retimed, runs in between two
southbound diverted WCML
expresses, thereby requiring a
spirited climb to Ais Gill. Class 40s
are the popular choice of motive
power for this train.

Plate 68 *(below)* At 06.55, and in
the summer sunshine, a Class 40,
No. 40 012 *Aureol* emerges from
Birkett Tunnel with a down freight
on 25th July 1980.

Plate 71 *(left, upper)* Wharton Hall, south of Kirkby Stephen, as a Class 45 swoops through with the 07.15 Nottingham—Glasgow express.

Plate 72 *(left, lower)* With the embankment on fire, Class 40, No. 40 091, climbs away from Kirkby Stephen West, with an 'up' cement train on 30th December 1977.

Plate 73 *(above)* Class 50, No. 50 029, silhouetted against the winter sunset, heads the 09.15 London Euston—Glasgow Central express south of Kirkby Stephen West on 12th January 1975.

Plate 74 *(below)* The 'Thames-Clyde Express' in its last year, complete with restaurant car, attacks the climb away from Kirkby Stephen West. Mallerstang Edge forms the background high above the village of Nateby.

Plate 75 *(above)* Winter sunshine breaks through as the first express of the day, travelling north, descends through Kirkby Stephen West.

Plate 76 *(left)* Early morning at Kirkby Stephen, as a Class 47 picks its way through 'wrong line' with the Derby—Glasgow 'Mondays only' e.c.s. train. A landslip south of Kirkby Stephen had necessitated single line working on this occasion.

Plate 77 Although extra Saturday trains and relief expresses are now uncommon over the Settle—Carlisle line, it is still possible to strike a lucky day. On such an occasion a Class 45 swings round Kirkby Stephen West's tall Down Home signal with an extra express for the north.

Plate 78 Activity in the modern signal box at Kirkby Stephen West. Signalman Walter Jackson is in charge.

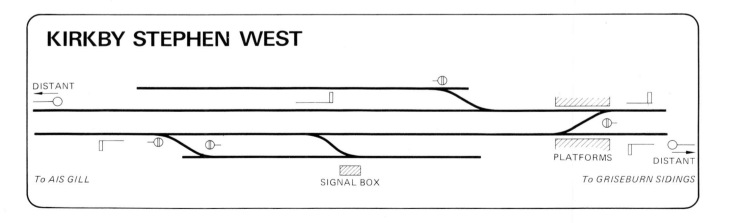

KIRKBY STEPHEN WEST

DISTANT

SIGNAL BOX

PLATFORMS

DISTANT

To AIS GILL

To GRISEBURN SIDINGS

Plate 79 *(right, upper)* The Kirkby Stephen relief signalman, Norman Guy, and the driver of the late running 10.25 Nottingham—Glasgow express discuss the problems associated with blizzard conditions and heavy snow drifting en route, during January 1979. ▶

Plate 80 *(right, lower)* No. 45 037 in the fog at Kirkby Stephen West on 23rd December 1978. Signalman Artie Richardson is in charge. ▶

Plate 83 *(above)* The old bridge over the A685 at Kirkby Stephen West.

Plate 81 *(left, upper)* Nos. 25 146 and 25 291, double-heading, in the appalling weather conditions common during the winter of January 1979, prepare to make a further trip from Kirkby Stephen, 'over the bank', on 20th January 1979, to keep this important route open.

Plate 82 *(left, lower)* Rare occurrence at Kirkby Stephen West. A Class 25 pilots a Class 40 on the Glasgow—Nottingham express, whilst another Class 25 trundles down the bank towards Appleby.

Plate 84 *(right)* The replacement of the overbridge at Kirkby Stephen West during the night. Two steam cranes were utilized, the duty being the last task for one of them, as they are being gradually replaced by new hydraulic units.

S. Steadman

Plate 87 *(right, upper)* No. 47 112 prepares to penetrate the rock cutting at Waitby, with a Saturday morning northbound car train, on 10th November 1979.

Plate 88 *(right, lower)* Making a spirited climb through Smardale, on 10th November 1979, is the lightweight six coach 09.35 Carlisle—Nottingham express.

Plate 85 *(left)* A short mixed freight trundles away from Kirkby Stephen West on Good Friday, 4th April 1980, with a Class 40 in charge.

Plate 86 *(below)* Class 40, No. 40 024 *Lucania* grinds past Waitby School at lunchtime on Good Friday, 4th April 1980.

Plate 89 *(above)* The beautiful curving Smardale Viaduct carrying the morning 'down' express on 10th November 1979.

Plate 90 *(left)* Sunset at Smardale, as a Class 25 climbs gently southward.

Plate 91 *(right, above)* A Class 47 ▶ swings away from Crosby Garrett with a 'down' express.

Plate 92 *(right, lower)* Evening at ▶ Stockber. Two Class 40s power their way towards Crosby Garrett, on 28th May 1980, with 7G02, an 'up' mixed freight from Carlisle.

Plate 93 *(above)* With a diverted East Coast Main Line freight, and travelling via the Settle—Carlisle route, due to the collapse of the Penmanshiel Tunnel, Class 40, No. 40 124, is seen here, south of Griseburn, and struggling to keep going.

Plate 94 *(left)* Single line working between Kirkby Stephen and Griseburn involved the stopping of all expresses on a particular Sunday in 1977. A Class 47, so affected, eases its train toward the crossover at Griseburn, with the linesman watching intently.

GRISEBURN BALLAST SIDING

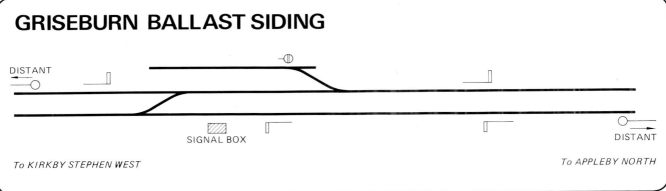

DISTANT

SIGNAL BOX

DISTANT

To KIRKBY STEPHEN WEST

To APPLEBY NORTH

Plate 95 *(above)* The excellently preserved signal box at Griseburn Ballast Sidings. Note the supply of coal for the box.

Plate 96 *(right)* On 31st July 1976, Class 45, No. 45 006 *Honourable Artillery Company* hurries through Griseburn with an 'up' excursion, hot on the heels of the regular express, behind No. 45 039 *The Manchester Regiment*, which had passed 15 minutes earlier.

Plate 97 *(left)* Climbing towards Griseburn, through Breaks Hall, on 23rd December 1979, with 1M24, the 09.25 Glasgow—Birmingham New Street express, is Class 47, No. 47 410, of Finsbury Park depot.

Plate 98 *(right)* On 23rd December 1979, Class 47, No. 47 469, exits from Helm Tunnel, with 1M42, the 11.05 Glasgow—London Euston express.

Plate 99 *(below)* Class 47, No. 47 501, eases 'The Western Border Venturer' into Helm Tunnel on 13th May 1978. This was a sad day for railway enthusiasts and railwaymen everywhere, as Bishop Eric Treacy died later that afternoon, whilst photographing *Evening Star* near Appleby station.

Plate 101 *(above)* Before the Class 45s supremacy on all Midland line expresses had been challenged, we see the evening 'up' express leave Helm Tunnel and begin the sweep round to Griseburn and the south.

Plate 102 *(right)* Driver Arthur Nicholson of Carlisle at the controls of Class 25, No. 25 156, bound for Carlisle, following the completion of a Sunday ballast working.

Plate 100 *(left)* Class 47, No. 47 538, drifts past Breaks Hall with 1S41, the 09.40 Liverpool Lime Street—Glasgow express, on 23rd December 1979.

Plate 103 *(left, upper)* On 14th April 1979, Class 40, No. 40 034, *Accra* accelerates IM86, the 11.50 Glasgow Central—Nottingham express towards Helm Tunnel and the south.

I. Welsh

Plate 104 *(left, lower)* With an 'up' relief express, Class 47, No. 47 424, attacks the 1 in 100 over Ormside Viaduct, on 1st June 1980. Cross Fell, complete with radar masts, can be seen in the background. The conical shaped mound in the foreground is Knock Pike.

Plate 105 *(right)* A regular feature of the Settle-Carlisle route, once West Coast Main Line trains have resumed their normal route over Shap during the summer, is Sunday engineering work. Class 25, No. 25 041 is pictured here on permanent way work near Ormside, on 25th May 1980.

Plate 106 *(below)* With a train of empty hopper wagons, Class 40, No. 40 170, trundles away from Ormside towards Appleby on 1st June 1980. The recently deposited ballast can be seen in the background.

Plate 107 *(above)* Loading ramps and ladders at Appleby West Goods Shed, despite the reference to Kirkby Thore. Alas, both ramps and the railway through Kirkby Thore are only a memory. Note the L.N.E.R. painted out and BR (E) repainted on top.

Plate 108 *(right)* The interior of Appleby West box, after removal of a surplus crossover, causing the spare levers (middle) evident in this picture. This box operated on a more or less continual 24 hour basis, from its construction until eventual demise in the early 1970s, when all Appleby operations were transferred to the North box, following closure of the goods yard.

Plate 109 *(below)* Appleby West signal box in the 1960s. Signalman Artie Richardson is in attendance.

Plate 110 *(right)* The goods yard at Appleby West, on the last day of operation in October 1971, with a freight waiting on the relief line.

Plate 111 *(below)* All quiet at Appleby in the evening. Gas lights, yard, signal box and train-men's cabin still remain in October 1971.

Plate 112 *(above)* No. 45 001 pauses briefly at Appleby with 1E80, a Carlisle—Sheffield relief express on 6th January 1980.

Plate 113 *(left)* Appleby's leading railwoman, Lynn Scott, hands over the cash bag to Skipton guard, Sid Brammer.

Plate 114 *(below)* Gordon Harris, a true railwayman and enthusiast who was lamp man on the line, now at Appleby station.

Plate 115 *(right, upper)* The end is in sight for shunters, Nos. D2706 and D2710 as they pause at Appleby on their way to the breakers' yard during the early/mid 1960s.

S. Steadman

Plate 116 *(right, lower)* Appleby West station 'down' side main buildings, as seen on 20th November 1979. Note the plaque in memory of Bishop Eric Treacy, who collapsed and died at Appleby station on 13th May 1978.

Plate 119 *(right, upper)* A very rare event indeed. The area steam crane at Warcop sidings, following the re-railing of some derailed goods vans.

Plate 120 *(right, lower)* The crane crossing the Sandford overbridge, still on the Warcop line.

Plate 117 *(left)* Lamps at Appleby. Lamps of various sizes and types at Appleby station.

Plate 118 *(below)* The 'down' express in the fog at Appleby, January 1980.

Plate 121 *(left)* It's now on the move, still in steam, with Class 25, No. 25 294 approaching the A66 overbridge at Appleby.

Plate 122 *(below)* Finally ready to leave for Carlisle.

Plate 123 *(above)* The Eden Valley Branch is disturbed on 20th May 1978 by Class 40, No. 40 118, on one of the infrequent troop specials to Warcop. The weed-grown track in the foreground is all that remains of this once famous route to Penrith. The head shunt to this small section has been further cut back to ease works on the Appleby by-pass.

Plate 124 *(below)* Appleby East signal box, now demolished, controlled the crossing to the north of Appleby East station. Note the different style of box construction.

Plate 125 *(below)* The interior of Appleby East signal box. The signalman, (the late Alf Smith), operates the gate lock. All the remaining levers were out of use by this time (1965). Alf was a 'Midland' man during his normal working life. He only operated Appleby East box, as required, on Mondays, Wednesdays and Fridays, during his semi-retirement, to allow passage of the Merrygill train.

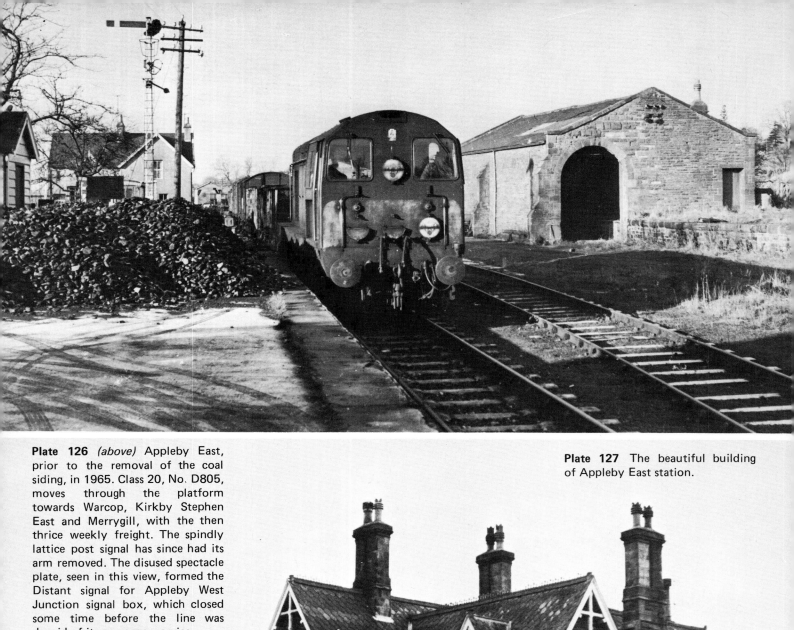

Plate 126 *(above)* Appleby East, prior to the removal of the coal siding, in 1965. Class 20, No. D805, moves through the platform towards Warcop, Kirkby Stephen East and Merrygill, with the then thrice weekly freight. The spindly lattice post signal has since had its arm removed. The disused spectacle plate, seen in this view, formed the Distant signal for Appleby West Junction signal box, which closed some time before the line was devoid of its passenger service.

Plate 127 The beautiful building of Appleby East station.

Plate 128   Class 25, No. 25 144, trundles away in a snow storm from Appleby East with the twice weekly (Wednesday and Friday) extension of the pick-up goods to Warcop, on 19th March 1980.

Plate 129 *(left, upper)* The only remaining NER Viaduct in use in Westmorland, at Coupland Beck, between Appleby East and Warcop.

Plate 130 *(left, lower)* The 'Warcop' freight returns through the gloom near New Hall, on 19th March 1980.

Plate 131 *(above)* Warcop station, now a private residence, still with station clock in position.

Plate 133 *(right)* Warcop signal box and a superb NER bracket signal.

Plate 132 *(lower)* The interior of Warcop signal box, when in use. Note the token apparatus.

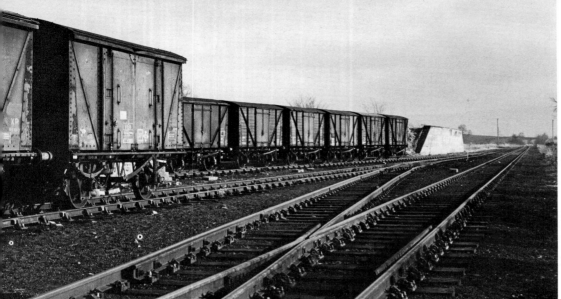

Plate 134 A healthy string of vans await collection at Warcop during March 1980. Much of the yard here was removed during the late 1960s. However, following the closure of the Warcop to Merrygill section, a new loop at Warcop was introduced complete with the re-instatement of two sidings.

Plate 135 On the closed, and now lifted, section of the line, the 'Warcop' approaches Musgrave.

Plate 136 The end for the Merrygill branch. A Class 25 trundles towards Musgrave from Kirkby Stephen East, on 31st October 1974, for the very last time.

Plate 137 *(right)* Driver Sullevan, of Carlisle depot, enjoys the early morning sunshine during gaps in the shunting at Appleby yard.

25 060

Class 25/1	
Weight tonnes	74
Brake force tonnes	38
ETH index	
RA	5
Max speed mph	90

Plate 138 *(below)* The exit from 'the branch' at Appleby North. A Class 40 powered engineers' train creeps towards the main line. The telephoto lens accentuates the unevenness of the track, whilst the buildings look as though 'squareness' was unheard of during their construction.

Plate 142 *(right, upper)* The cluster of old cabins which comprise the 'Engineers' behind Appleby North signal box.

Plate 143 and **144** *(right, lower)* Permanent Way department buildings of different construction at Appleby.

Plate 139 *(left)* Appleby North signal box, warm and inviting in the cold winter's night air.

Plate 140 *(left, lower)* The late Joe Eggleston at work in the box at Appleby North, prior to replacement of the attractive wood and brass rotary block instruments. Extra levers were added to the frame in Appleby North box when Appleby West box closed.

Plate 141 *(below)* 01.10 in Appleby North box, all quiet but for the popping of the gas light. Perhaps one night the Kirkby Stephen signalman will bell through a compound on a night 'Scotch'!

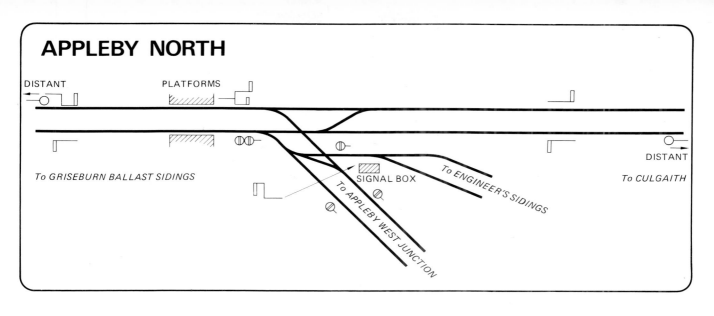

APPLEBY NORTH

DISTANT   PLATFORMS

To GRISEBURN BALLAST SIDINGS

SIGNAL BOX

To APPLEBY WEST JUNCTION

To ENGINEER'S SIDINGS

DISTANT

To CULGAITH

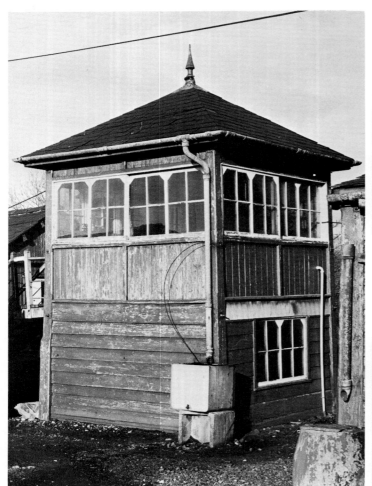

Plate 145 *(above)* The signal and telegraph department cabin at Appleby, in the shape of an old signal box.

Plate 146 *(right)* The Works Department building at Appleby, with many useful pieces lying around.

Plate 147 *(upper, right)* Tom's cabin. This structure, which was, regrettably, demolished only two or three years ago, stood in the northern area of the 'Engineers' yard at Appleby. It has been rumoured that this cabin was an original 'navvies' dwelling.

Plate 148 *(right)* The gang at Appleby.

P. Holden

Plate 149 *(upper)* A diverted 'up' East Coast Main Line express passes the entrance to the Engineers' Sidings at Appleby. The telephoto lens produces an interesting view of the trackwork.

Plate 150 *(below)* Fearsome snows and associated conditions were encountered during the winter of 1978/79. The ploughs prepare to leave Appleby on another mission in March 1979, in an effort to keep the route open. *P. Holden*

Plate 153 *(right, upper)* A diverted ECML 'down' freight trundles past Brampton Road Ends.

Plate 154 *(right, lower)* Long Marton Viaduct carries the late running morning 'down' express, with a Class 40 assisting a failed Class 45.

Plate 151 *(left)* The difficulties experienced at Appleby North, especially by trains leaving Appleby for Carlisle with the combined, and sometimes lengthy, Warcop/Merrygill/Kirkby Stephen East trains, were caused by the poor siting of Appleby North's Down Starter. Generations of signalmen have struggled with trains blocking both main lines whilst waiting for the road to Carlisle. Goods traffic at Appleby has now ceased, and the 'Warcop' rarely consists of more than a few vans; the signal has been moved to a more convenient position. The old signal is seen here prior to demolition.

Plate 152 *(below)* The exit from Appleby to the North is flanked by telegraph poles and signals, as a Class 45 powers away from the platforms with a northbound express.

Plate 155 *(left)* Long Marton 'up' side main station building, following complete closure, but prior to the removal of platform edging. This station is now a centre for a Lancashire school, and is still in fairly good condition.

Plate 156 *(below)* Seabirds fly across the path of Class 47, No. 47 131, as it nears Hale Grange overbridge, with the afternoon Glasgow—Nottingham express on 11th April 1980.

Plate 157 *(above)* Class 20s are frequent visitors to the Settle—Carlisle line, in the form of dead engines being taken to and from the works at Glasgow. No. 20 041 forms part of a northbound freight being hauled by No. 40 185, on 19th March 1980, near McGhies Siding, Kirkby Thore.

Plate 158 *(right)* McGhies ground frame at the British Gypsum factory near Kirkby Thore, with some new trackwork being installed.

Plate 159 *(above)* On 25th October 1979, the 'Deltic Railtour', which was organised by the Locomotive Club of Great Britain, accelerated through Hale Grange. This tour helped to mark a welcome return for 'Deltic' No. 55 016 *Gordon Highlander*, which, some weeks previously, had been languishing in Doncaster Works, with its future uncertain.

Plate 160 *(left)* The pleasant building at Newbiggin, unfortunately disused and rapidly deteriorating, photographed in the evening sun.

Plate 161 *(right, upper)* Super-power at Newbiggin. Class 40s, Nos. 40 008 and 40 181 head south with an early morning freight.

S. Steadman

Plate 162 *(right, lower)* On 14th May 1978, standing on the wrong line at Newbiggin with an engineers' train, is Class 37, No. 37 200.

CULGAITH STATION

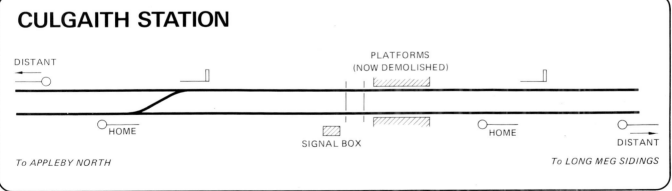

◄ **Plate 163** *(left, upper)* Freezing conditions, south of Culgaith, on 24th December 1979, as No. 45 019 passes with the afternoon 'down' express.

Plate 165 *(above)* Culgaith signal box, and its crossing gates, standing right by the road.

◄ **Plate 164** *(left, lower)* A Class 47 pilots a Class 50 on a 'down' WCML diverted express through the rain at Culgaith. Note the remains of the loading gauge on the right.

Plate 166 *(above)* Inspector Jimmy Calder enters Culgaith signal box, whilst Class 37, No. 37 200 waits on the 'down' line, on the crossing, outside.

Plate 167 *(left)* The barrier control at Culgaith is operated by signalman Alan Dugdale, who was formerly signalman at Carlisle Upperby and Southwaite, prior to its closure.

Plate 168 *(right, upper)* Now as regular over the Settle— Carlisle route as Holbeck 'Royal Scots' used to be, No. 45 073 wanders through Culgaith with the afternoon 'up' express on 24th December 1979.

Plate 169 *(right, lower)* Class 46, No. 46 053, races toward the tunnels to the north of Culgaith with the afternoon Glasgow Central—Nottingham express.

Plate 170 *(left, upper)* Running through the easily graded stretch between Langwathby and Culgaith, on 27th October 1979, is Class 47, No. 47 457. The train is the afternoon 'up' scheduled express.

Plate 171 *(left, lower)* Langwathby station, seen here in 1966, is typical of the style of buildings seen on the line.

Plate 172 *(above)* Class 40, No. 40 109, on a 'down' mixed freight, proceeds quietly through Langwathby on 20th March 1980.

Plate 173 *(below)* The fast stretch between Langwathby and Little Salkeld. A northbound express speeds by in the care of a Class 45 on 7th April 1980.

Plate 174 *(above)* The clock, still working, at Little Salkeld station. Note the detailed woodwork, characteristic of the stations along the line.

Plate 175 *(above)* Small bridge for a water course at Long Meg, local stone having been used for its construction.

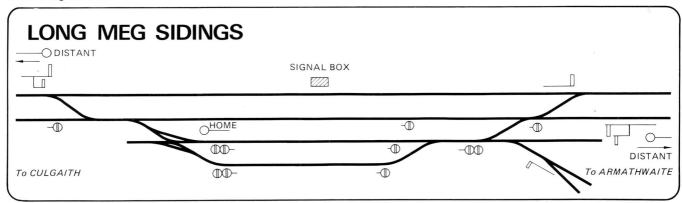

LONG MEG SIDINGS

○ DISTANT

SIGNAL BOX

HOME

DISTANT

To CULGAITH

To ARMATHWAITE

Plate 176 *(below)* A useful photograph showing the signal box, sidings and signals at Long Meg.

Plate 177 *(above)* Further down the line, one can see the sidings disappear to the right, and the wall mounted ground discs.

Plate 179 *(right)* A view in the opposite direction looking from the throat of the sidings.

Plate 178 *(below)* It's lamp time at Long Meg.

Plate 182 *(above)* Class 47, No. 47 045, coasting through the Eden Valley, over Eden Lacy Viaduct, with the 'Travellers Fare' centenary excursion on 22nd September 1979.

Plate 183 *(right)* Although never used, we can still see the 'down' side water crane at Lazonby in 1980.

◀ **Plate 180** *(left, upper)* Double-headed Class 40s, on a rail train, wait on the inside loop at Long Meg.

◀ **Plate 181** *(left, lower)* As the mist begins to rise, a Class 40 slips over the Eden Lacy Viaduct.

Plate 184 *(left, upper)* Class 31s, Nos. 31 246 and 31 270 sweep away towards Chesterfield from Armathwaite with a returning football excursion on 5th April 1981.

Plate 185 *(left, lower)* Morning mist rising from the hoar frost, still clings to the arches of the viaduct at Armathwaite, as the 'down' morning express crosses on 28th December 1979.

Plate 186 *(right)* An underbridge at Armathwaite, showing an unusual style of architecture for the line.

Plate 187 *(below)* HST unit, No. 254 025, on a British Rail Board photographic excursion, accelerates over Armathwaite Viaduct and away to the south on 10th November 1979. High Speed sets are still a rarity over the Settle—Carlisle route.

Plate 188 *(above)* Class 47, No. 47 429, negotiates the curves through Armathwaite with the morning 'down' express on 20th March 1980. A change in working patterns became evident in the early 1980s, whereby Class 45s and 47s seem to have supplanted Class 40s on all regular passenger working over the line.

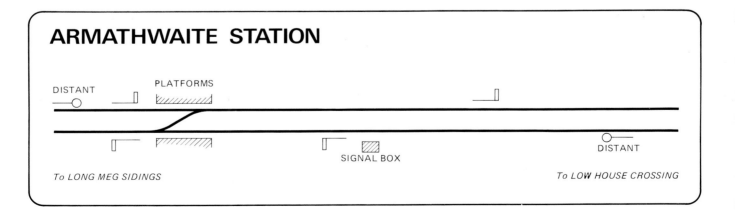

ARMATHWAITE STATION

DISTANT

PLATFORMS

SIGNAL BOX

DISTANT

To LONG MEG SIDINGS

To LOW HOUSE CROSSING

Plate 189 *(above)* The rather tall structure of Armathwaite signal box.

Plate 190 *(right)* Signalman Jack Hall enters the passage of a 'down' light engine, No. 37 246, into the train register in Armathwaite box on 10th November 1979. The clock came from one of the closed boxes on the West Coast Main Line.

Plate 191 *(left)* The block instrument shelf and signal levers, inside the box which controls the simple layout at this point.

Plate 192 *(above)* Class 25, No. 25 041, near Drybeck Viaduct, makes its way back to the yard at Kingmoor, with the pick-up goods on 20th March 1980.

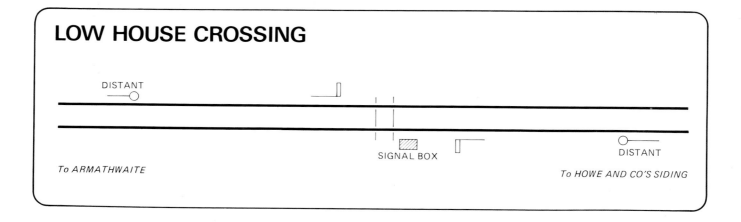

LOW HOUSE CROSSING

DISTANT

SIGNAL BOX

DISTANT

To ARMATHWAITE

To HOWE AND CO'S SIDING

Plate 193 *(above)* Low House Crossing box.

Plate 194 *(right)* The block instrument shelf in the Low House Crossing box.

Plate 199 *(above)* Heading an afternoon 'down' freight past an 'up' express through Low House on 8th November 1977, is Class 47, No. 47 238.

Plate 200 *(right)* Almost all signs of railway involvement, apart from railway dwellings, have disappeared from Cotehill. Class 25, No. 25 214, heads north through the site of the station on 8th November 1977.

◄ **Plate 195** *(left, upper left)* The complete inside of this small compact box.

◄ **Plate 196** *(left, upper right)* Alan Dugdale, in Low House box, entering up the train register.

◄ **Plate 197** *(left, lower left)* Conversation in Low House box. Dickie Birtle and Clarrie Davidson, signalmen, putting the day's problems right.

◄ **Plate 198** *(left, lower right)* The lamp cabin at Low House, with its fine Midland Railway cast iron sign alongside.

Plate 201 *(above)* Howe & Co's. Siding signal box, lamp hut and platelayers residence.

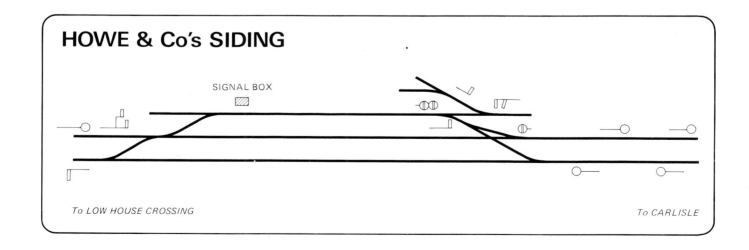

HOWE & Co's SIDING

SIGNAL BOX

To LOW HOUSE CROSSING

To CARLISLE

Plates 202 *(right)* and **203** *(below)* Signalman Eddie Foster awaits the passage of the pick-up through Howe & Co's. Sidings, on 28th December 1979. A few minutes later, Class 25, No. 25 318 obliged.

Plate 204 *(above)* Powering through Howe & Co's. Sidings with an 'up' freight en route for Severn Tunnel Junction on 28th December 1979, is Class 40, No. 40 008, of Carlisle Kingmoor depot.

Plate 205 *(left)* In an exceedingly overgrown state are Howe & Co's. Sidings, with the box in the background.

Plate 206 *(right, upper)* Threading the 1330 Glasgow—Nottingham express through the untidy area between Carlisle Citadel station and the open country to the south, is Class 47, No. 47 433.

Plate 207 *(right, below)* The well preserved station buildings at Cumwhinton in March 1980.

HOWE & CO'S SIDING

Plate 208 *(above)* 1M88 was the reporting code for 'The Waverley' express. This now withdrawn famous train is shown preparing to leave Carlisle behind 'Peak' No. D15, later renumbered 45 018, on 24th July 1963.

B. Cooper

Plate 209 *(left)* No. 45 002 takes water for its boiler at Carlisle, prior to the run to Appleby, Settle and the south.

Plate 210 *(right, above)* An unidentified 'Peak' at Carlisle Citadel Station, awaiting the 'off' from Platform 4 with a train for Settle.

Plate 211 *(right, below)* Class 40, No. 40 042 stands with its underframe packed with snow at the north end of Carlisle Citadel station (Platform No. 4) after successfully reaching Carlisle with the morning express. Weather conditions over Ais Gill were atrocious on 17th March 1979.

◀ Plate 212 *(left, upper)* Always waiting. Kingmoor Steam Crane.

◀ Plate 213 *(left, lower)* The scene inside Carlisle Kingmoor diesel maintenance depot, which is 'home' for many Settle—Carlisle engines.

Appendix One

OUTLINE OF PASSENGER SERVICES, SETTLE—CARLISLE ON NORMAL WEEKDAYS

Nottingham Midland	0715	1025	1605
Sheffield Midland	0813	1125	1703
Leeds City	0920	1230	1807
Keighley	0943	1253	1830
Skipton	0956	1308	1843
Appleby West	1101	1415	1948
Carlisle	1140	1455	2027
Glasgow Central	1359	1626	

The 0715 and 1025 departures from Nottingham both convey Buffet cars

Glasgow Central		1150	1610
Carlisle	0935	1322	1827
Appleby West	1014	1401	1905
Settle	1106	1455	1956
Skipton	1125	1515	2015
Keighley	1136		2025
Leeds City	1159	1548A	2048B
Sheffield Midland	1303	1653	2152
Nottingham Midland	1417	1753	2303

A — Passengers for London change at Leeds, dept 1645 arr Kings Cross 1904.

B — Passengers for London change at Leeds, dept 2200 arr Kings Cross 0158

The 1150 and 1610 departures from Glasgow Central both convey Buffet cars

Full, authoritative timetable information for Scotland—Midlands—London travel via the Settle—Carlisle can be obtained from the British Rail official timetables tables 37, 65, 26 and 53.

Appendix Two

OUTLINE OF 'DALESRAIL' OPERATIONS, SETTLE—CARLISLE.
(Selected Summer Saturdays only)

Preston	0845	—
Bamber Bridge	0854	—
Blackpool	—	1730
Blackburn	0908	—
Clitheroe	0926	1836
Hellifield		1913
Settle	1034	1923 C
Horton	1049	1936
Ribblehead	—	— A
Dent	1106	1955
Garsdale	1115	2003
Kirkby Stephen	1130	2017
Appleby	1142	2028
Langwathby	1159	2045
Lazonby	1208	2053
Armathwaite	1218	2103
Carlisle	1235	2119
Carlisle	0830	1715
Armathwaite	0850	1733
Lazonby	0859	1744
Langwathby	0908	1755
Appleby	0926	1813
Kirkby Stephen	0945	1832
Garsdale	1002	1850
Dent	1010	1857
Ribblehead	1018	1908
Horton	1026	1916
Settle	1035 B	1926
Hellifield	1043	1937
Clitheroe	1104	1959
Blackburn	—	2018
Bamber Bridge	—	2029
Blackpool	1221	—
Preston	—	2038

Note:

A — Ribblehead Station open for southbound trains only.

B— Passengers for Leeds, Bradford, Skipton, Keighley change at Settle.
Passengers for Bingley and Shipley change at Settle and Keighley.

C— Passengers from all stations covered by note 'B' change at Settle for
Horton and the north.

Full, authoritative timetable and fares information can be obtained from British Rail stations.

The information above has been compiled from various 'Dalesrail' leaflets, kindly supplied by the Yorkshire Dales National Park.

Appendix Three

Of interest to time recording enthusiasts, this log illustrates the performance of a 'Peak' Class diesel in the heyday of Settle—Carlisle diesel-hauled expresses running: Saturday 22nd June, 1963, 2.38pm Leeds—Carlisle—Glasgow 'The Thames—Clyde Express'. Locomotive No. D156, 2,500hp 'Peak'. Load: 11 coaches, including buffet and restaurant car, equalling 388/410 tons. Weather: Fine and dry but with side wind. Reason for late start due to late arrival in and failure of diesel locomotive. Do not know if No. D156 was the locomotive that failed or if new locomotive, however, 23 minutes late start was reduced to 3 minutes late arrival.

Log by Brian Cooper

DISTANCE MILES			SCHED. MIN	ACTUAL M. S.	SPEEDS m.p.h.	
0.0	Leeds City		0	0	0	3.01 28PM (2.38PM)
	Whitehall Jc.	(D)		2. 10		
	Holbeck L.L.			2. 35		
1.7	Armley			3. 55	49.2	
	Kirkstall			5. 33	66.2	
4.6	Newlay &			6. 53	62.0	
	Calverley			8. 08	65.8	
	Apperley Jc.	(U)		9. 04	78.9	
7.6	Apperley Bdg.			9. 44	64.8	
		203		9. 59	64.8	
	Thackley Jc.	(D)		11. 41	40.9	205—11.53 Brakes 20PWS
10.7	Leeds Jc.	(D)		13. 40	—	PWS 20 m.p.h.
		206		14. 05	38.1	
	Saltaire			15. 06	48.6	
		207		15. 26	53.6	
		208		16. 30	59.7	
13.8	Bingley			17. 16	65.8	
		210		18. 22	67.2	
	Marley Jc.	(D)		18. 44	68.2	
		211		19. 15	69.8	
	Thwaites Jc.	(U)		19. 41	57.4	
17.0	Keighley			20. 18	57.4	
		213		21. 18	58.1	
		214		22. 14	67.2	
20.0	Steeton			23. 12	67.7	
		216		24. 01	66.2	
	Kildwick			24. 50	68.2	
		218		25. 46	71.0	
23.1	Cononley			25. 59	71.0	
		219		26. 36	72.6	
	Snaygill	(D)	35	27. 28	67.7	Brake for PWS
26.2	Skipton		36½	28. 56	50.0	Slack
	Skipton N. Jc.	(D)		29. 33	53.3	
		223		30. 53	58.4	
	Delaney Sdg.	(U)		31. 35	60.8	
		224		31. 52	61.2	
29.9	Gargrave			32. 51	60.8	
		226		33. 51	60.4	
		227		34. 50	62.5	
	Bellbusk			35. 30	61.4	Brake ?
	Summit 229½			38. 23	27.9	
		230		39. 13	40.5	
		231		40. 22	58.4	
36.2	Hellifield		48	40. 41	63.9	
		232		41. 18	66.7	
	Long Preston			41. 44	73.2	
		233		42. 09	73.2	
		234		42. 59	72.0	
39.5	Settle Jc.	(D)	51	43. 25	68.2	Slack
		235		43. 51	68.2	
		236		44. 46	62.5	
	Settle			45. 16	62.0	
		237		45. 45	59.5	
		238	3	46. 47	57.4	
	Stainforth Sdg.	(U)		47. 05	57.4	
		239		47. 53	54.5	
		240		49. 00	52.8	
	Helwith Bdg.	(U)		50. 03	52.8	241—50.09
		242		51. 16	52.9	
47.4	Horton			51. 53	52.4	
		243		52. 42	51.8	
		244		53. 35	52.4	
	Sellside	(D)		54. 36	49.8	
		246		56. 01	48.6	
		247		57. 15	49.5	
52.2	Ribblehead			57. 33	49.2	
		248		58. 27	48.6	
53.4	Blea Moor	(U)	75½	59. 03	48.6	
		249		59. 41	48.6	

DISTANCE MILES			SCHED. MIN	ACTUAL M. S.	SPEEDS m.p.h.	
	Tun. Entrance			60. 06	48.6	2
	Tun. Exit			61. 42	64.8	258—61.53
	Dent Head	(D)		62. 17	66.2	
		252		62. 48	67.2	253—63.41—68.2
58.3	Dent			64. 14	66.7	254—64.34
	Tun. Entrance			64. 41	66.7	
	Tun. Exit			65. 15	72.6	
61.6	Garsdale	256	2	66. 14	73.2	
				66. 46	75.7	
		257		67. 03	77.6	
		258		67. 53	72.6	
		259		68. 45	64.8	
64.6	Ais Gill	(D)	88	69. 25	63.4	
		261		70. 35	70.4	Flanging
		262		71. 25	75.7	
		263		72. 11	80.4	
68.1	Mallerstang	(U)		72. 24	80.4	Brake Slightly
		264		72. 56	79.8	
		265		73. 40	82.6	Brake Slightly
		266		74. 23	83.4	
71.5	Kirkby Stephen			74. 50	78.3	
		267		75. 09	81.1	Brake Slightly
		268		75. 56	71.5	
		269		76. 46	69.8	
		271		78. 31	69.3	
	Griseburn	(U)		79. 20	69.8	
		273		80. 14	74.4	
		274		81. 01	78.3	
79.7	Ormside			81. 37	80.4	
		276		82. 33	73.2	
		277		83. 26	68.2	
82.2	Appleby		103½	83. 40	68.2	
		278		84. 19	67.2	
		279		85. 10	74.4	
85.1	Long Marton			86. 06	78.3	
		282		87. 30	76.3	
		283		88. 19	77.0	
88.3	Newbiggin			88. 35	76.3	
	Culgaith			89. 06	78.9	
		284		89. 59	79.8	
		286		90. 36	78.9	
		287		91. 23	77.6	
		288		92. 10	77.6	
93.2	Langwathby			92. 24	77.0	
		289		92. 58	79.8	
	Little Salkeld			93. 29	82.6	
		291		94. 24	81.1	
		292		95. 12	78.3	
97.5	Lazonby	(CLD)		95. 40	76.3	
		293		95. 58	78.3	
		294		96. 45	75.0	
99.9		295		97. 36	71.2	
		296		98. 24	78.3	
		297		99. 10	82.6	
		298		99. 55	77.6	
103.0	Armathwaite			100. 00	77.6	
		299		100. 42	76.3	
104.6	Low House	(U)		101. 16	68.7	
		300		101. 33	63.9	
		301		102. 29	66.7	
		302		103. 22	68.7	
	Howes Sdg.	(D)		104. 10	68.2	
		304		105. 18	64.3	
	Cumwhinton			105. 18	64.3	
		305		106. 07	64.8	
110.3	Scotby	(CLD)		106. 26	66.2	
112.1	Petterill Bdg. Jc.	(D)		109. 04	31.0	
113.0	Carlisle		131	110. 30	0	4.51

Appendix Four

DIVERTED WEST COAST MAIN LINE EXPRESSES, SUNDAYS, 1978

2330	SO	Euston — Glasgow Central	Appleby passing time 0548½
0940		Liverpool Lime Street — Glasgow Central	Appleby passing time 1308½
0915		Euston — Glasgow Central	Appleby passing time 1510

. . . .

0728		Carlisle — Euston	Appleby passing time 0806½
0900		Glasgow Central — Euston	Appleby passing time 1141
0925		Glasgow Central — Birmingham New Street	Appleby passing time 1217
0847		Glasgow Central — Red Bank Empty Vans	Appleby passing time 1240
1105		Glasgow Central — Euston	Appleby passing time 1344½

Appendix Five

SETTLE—CARLISLE SIGNAL BOXES

* Settle Junction
* Settle Station
  Stainforth Sidings
  Helwith Bridge
* Horton
  Selside
  Ribblehead
* Blea Moor
  Dent Head
* Dent Station
* Garsdale
* Ais Gill
  Mallerstang
* Kirkby Stephen West
  Crosby Garrett
* Griseburn Ballast Sidings
  Ormside
  Appleby West
* Appleby North
  Long Marton
  Newbiggin
* Culgaith
  Langwathby
  Little Salkeld
* Long Meg
  Lazonby
* Armathwaite
* Low House Crossing
  Cotehill
  Cumwhinton
* Howe & Co's. Siding
  Scotby
  Durranhill South
  Durranhill Junction
  Peterill Bridge Junction

* Denotes that these boxes were still in use at 1st
March 1980